Australia

THE JOURNEY SERIES

Photography by **Steven Nowakowski**
Text by Stella Martin

Front Cover: Dying light over the West MacDonnell Ranges, N.T.
Back Cover: The crystal clear waters of Whitehaven Beach, Whitsundays, Qld.
Inside Covers: The old rustic Hebel Hotel, Qld.

Dedicated to a new star in our life, our new daughter Stella.

steven nowakowski
PUBLISHING

Published by **Steven Nowakowski Publishing**
PO Box 4761 Cairns Queensland 4870 Australia
E: info@stevennowakowski.com
W: www.stevennowakowski.com

ISBN 978-0-9805002-4-0
© Steven Nowakowski Publishing 2011

Graphic design by Cameron LeBherz   www.lebherz.com.au

All rights reserved. No part of this publication may be reproduced (except brief passages for the purpose of a review), stored in a retrieval system or transmitted in any form or by any means, electronic, mechanical, photocopying, recording or otherwise, without the prior written permission of the publisher.

Introduction - a great southern land — 4

A land girt by sea — 20

Rainforests — 38

The red centre — 52

60,000 years of Aboriginal culture expressed in song and dance.

A great southern land

Australia has a long history. Some of the oldest rocks known on the planet belong to this island continent and while much of Europe was locked under ice, the first Australians were decorating cave walls with elaborate artworks.

This land is as diverse as it is vast. Running along the east coast, the Great Dividing Range draws rain from prevailing winds, channelling it back to the sea through rushing rivers and waterfalls. Rolling farmland clothes the gentler slopes but higher, southern peaks attract a generous coating of snow while in the tropical north dense rainforest covers the mountainsides.

Deprived of rainfall, the arid heart of Australia is home to some of the country's starkest and most stunning landscapes – baking deserts, rust-red ranges, hidden waterholes and dry riverbeds. The northern savannas are subjected to extremes: drought and fire in the winter months and inundation by summer monsoon rains when rivers spread across the landscape, filling wetlands and sparking a new cycle of life.

Separated from other land masses for about 35 million years, the flora and fauna of Australia evolved in isolation to produce a unique wildlife: over 80% of mammals and the majority of flowering plants are found nowhere else in the world. Australia is a very special place.

Clockwise: School wall mural in Kulumburu, W.A.; James Price Point, Kimberley Coastline, W.A., Rock art in Carnarvon Gorge, Qld, Kimberley children hitching a ride, W.A.

Overleaf: Hundred-year-old grass trees have survived the most extreme conditions on the western slopes of the Bunya Mountains, Qld.

The Kimberley region of north-west Australia is as large as most countries. It is one of the largest undisturbed tropical regions left on earth. These boab trees are a distinctive feature of the Kimberley. They are related to African baobab trees but no one knows how they reached Australia.

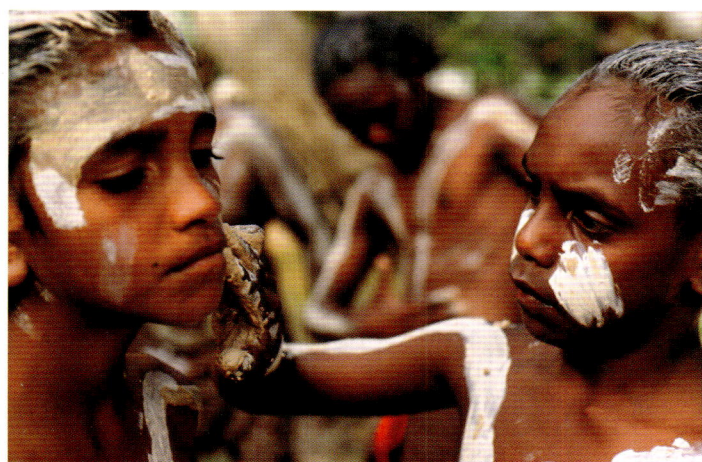

Clockwise: Aboriginal children preparing for dance; Eastern Grey Kangaroo; morning mist near Blencoe Falls, Qld.

Clockwise: Hopetoun Falls in the Otway Forests of Victoria; Arlington Reef off Cairns, Qld; another beautiful day at Fingal Bay, NSW.

Opposite: The Hinchinbrook Channel contains some of the richest diversity of marine plants in Australia and is home to some of the rarest marine animals such as the Snubfin Dolphin and the Flatback Turtle.

Rural south-east Queensland.

Overleaf: The highest peak in Victoria, Mt. Bogong.

Left: Rainforest meets reef, Cape Tribulation, Qld.
Right: Licuala Fan Palms, the Daintree lowland rainforests, Qld.

Left: Mitchell Falls, the Kimberley, W.A.
Right: Rock art in the Kimberley, W.A.

Overleaf: Still morning waters off Whitehaven Beach, Whitsundays, Qld.

17

A land girt by sea

Australia is surrounded by over 30,000km of coastline. Endless sandy beaches and rolling surf, rocky headlands and precipitous cliffs, mangroves and coral reefs fringe this vast island.

Roughly 80% of Australians live within 50km of the sea. The lives of Sydneysiders revolve around its magnificent harbour with the famous bridge and opera house. Beach-going here is a social occasion but, for those who seek solitude, Australia has no shortage of pristine, deserted beaches, some stretching for over 100km.

In the north, warm, tropical seas foster the growth of coral reefs, the most complex and diverse ecosystems on earth. The Great Barrier Reef shadows the Queensland coastline for 2,300km and is home to over 1,500 species of fish and countless other animals, each more colourful than the last. Nearly 1,000 islands and sand cays complete this tropical paradise. On the opposite side of the continent, Ningaloo Reef hugs part of the Western Australian coast, just a lazy paddle through turquoise waters from blindingly white sand beaches.

Southern coasts, under attack from the pounding waves of the Southern Ocean, are in retreat. In South Australia, the vast, arid Nullarbor Plain ends abruptly in cliffs that plunge into the Great Australian Bight; further east, the gigantic limestone rock stacks of Victoria's Twelve Apostles make a last dramatic stand.

Left: The iconic Sydney Opera House and Harbour Bridge are now world class monuments and a must-see destination.

Sculptured sandstone lines Sydney Harbour.

Pure white silica sands of Whitehaven Beach, Whitsundays, Qld.

Overleaf: A Sydney ferry turning into Circular Quay.

Bondi Beach is a playground for Sydneysiders.

Early morning on Whitehaven Beach, Qld.

Overleaf: Agincourt Reef off Port Douglas, Qld.

Previous spread: Twelve Apostles, Victoria.

Sparkling waters off Whitehaven Beach, Whitsundays, Qld.

Left: Low Isles off Port Douglas, Qld.
Right: The wreck of the Maheno on Fraser Island's Seventy-five Mile Beach, Qld.

Left: Southern Victoria's harsh and rugged coastline.
Right: Snorkelling the Whitsundays in Queensland.

Overleaf: First light at the historic town of 1770, Qld.

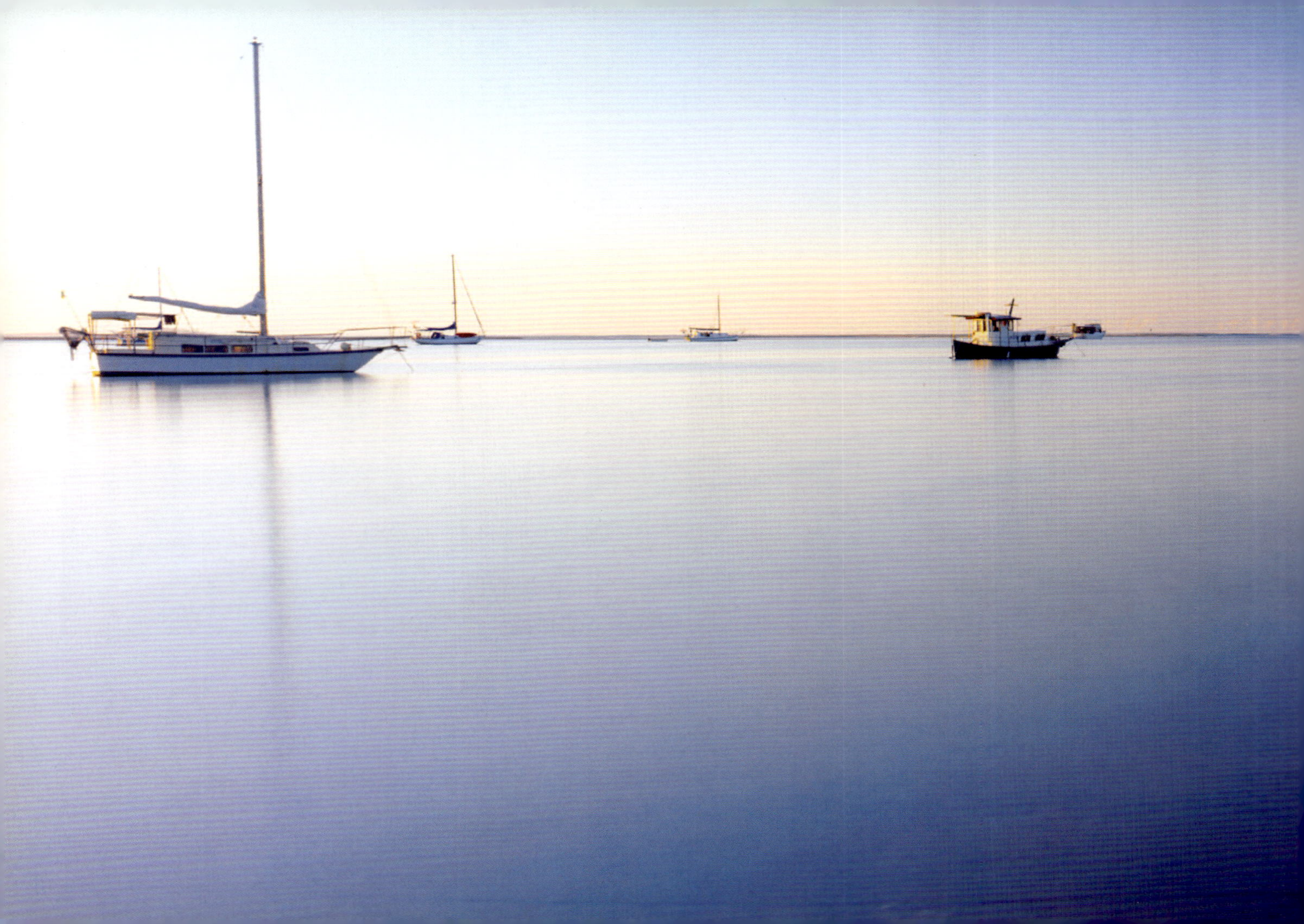

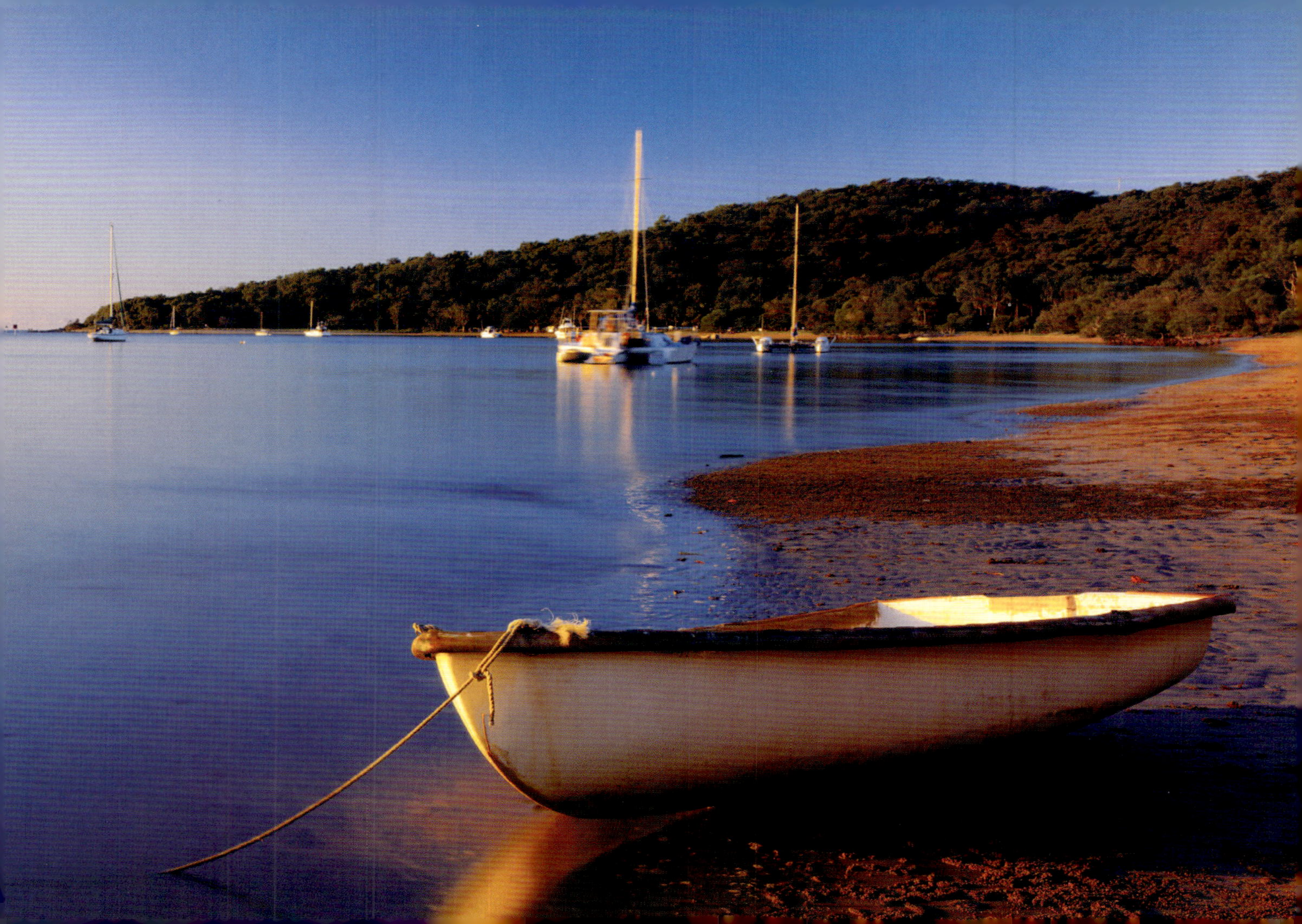

Coomera Falls in Green Mountains National Park, Qld.

Rainforests

Long ago, when Australia was part of the supercontinent of Gondwana, rainforest covered the land but, as the climate dried, it was forced to retreat to pockets on the relatively moist east coast. This remnant now covers just 3% of Australia – but is home to about half of all the country's plant families and about a third of mammal and half of bird species.

Competition in the rainforest is not for water but for sunlight. Forest giants stretch up on massive trunks, supported at the base by flanged buttresses. Other plants cheat – vines wind their way up to the sunlight using others for support while orchids and ferns squat on high tree branches. The result is an exuberant tangle of growth.

North Queensland's Wet Tropics World Heritage Area protects the country's largest continuous area of tropical rainforest, the most complex form. Further south, where the climate is wet, but cooler, temperate rainforest takes over. The gnarled, moss-covered trunks of Antarctic and myrtle beeches lend these forests a primordial atmosphere. Indeed, these trees differ little from their Gondwanan ancestors and individuals, sprouting from secondary stems when the main trunk dies, can be several thousand years old. Rainforests are the guardians of Australia's natural heritage.

Clockwise: Rainforest detail in the Jamieson Valley, Blue Mountains, NSW; lowland rainforest in north Queensland; Australia's highest single drop waterfall, Wallaman Falls, Qld.

Overleaf: Nandroya Falls within the Wet Tropics World Heritage Area, Qld.

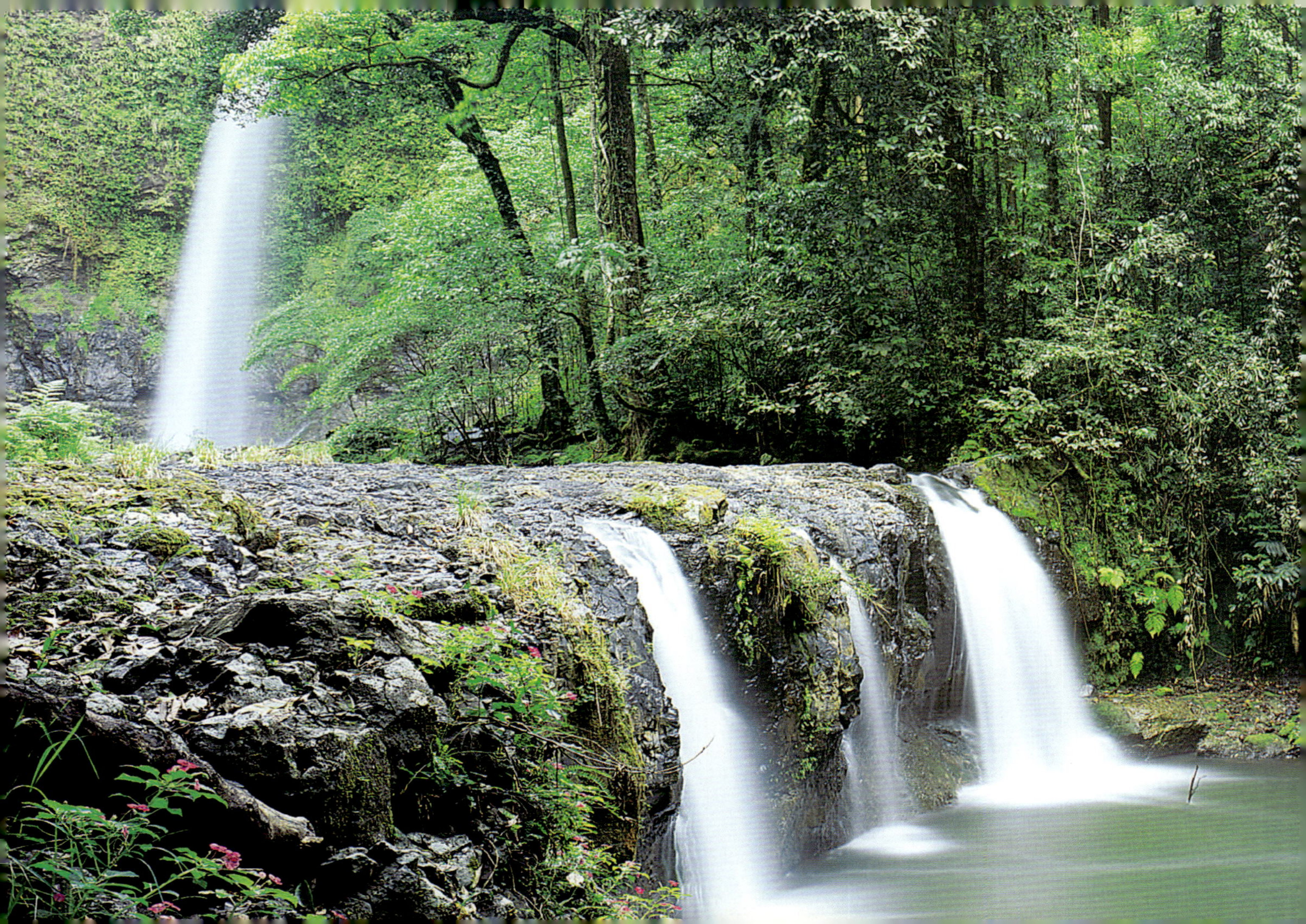

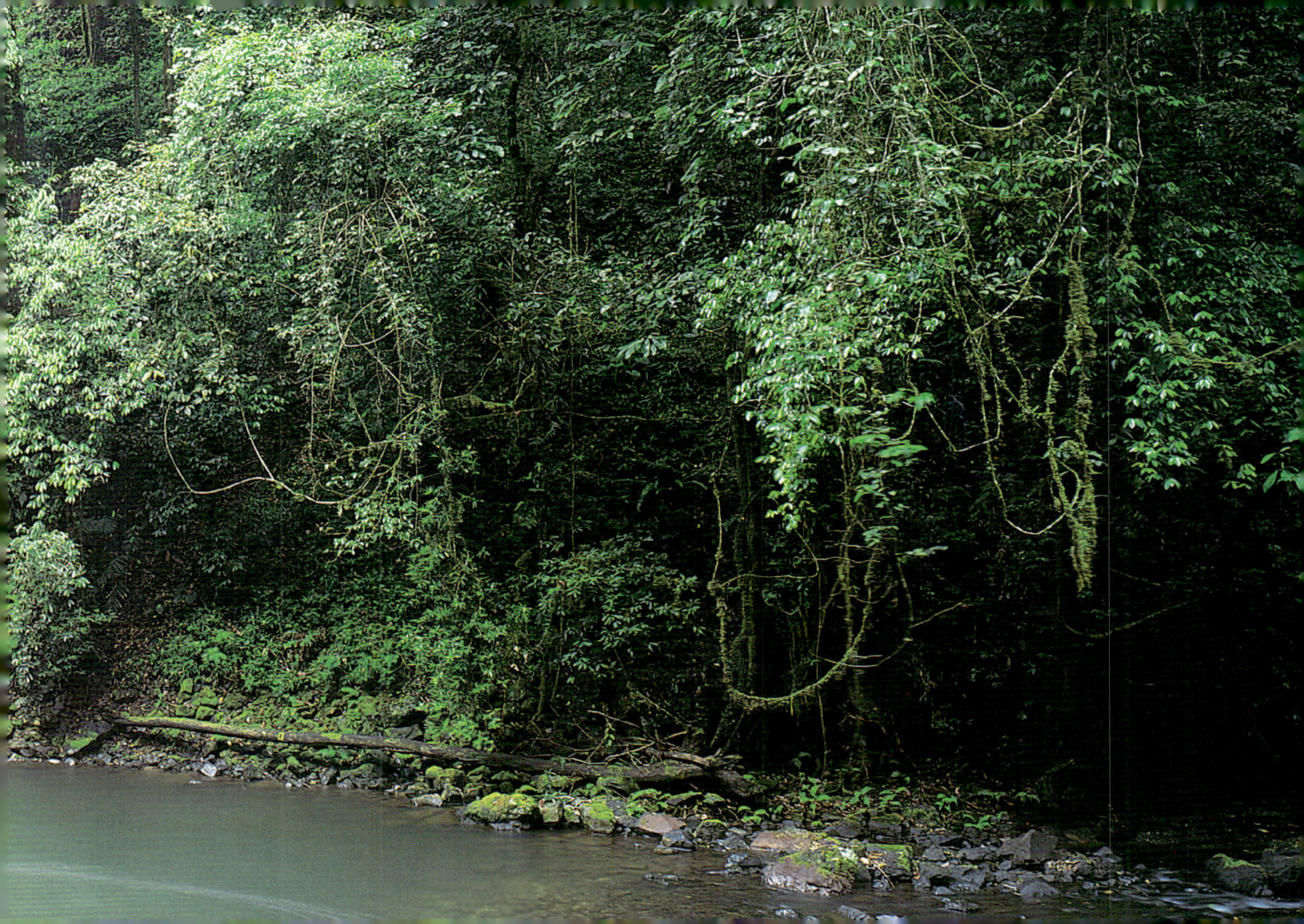

Clockwise: Millaa Millaa Falls, Qld; Northern Dwarf Tree Frog, Qld; Orange-thighed Tree Frog is found only in the Wet Tropics.

The shedding bark of these Tasmanian snow gums reveals their colourful trunks. These trees are the most cold-tolerant of the eucalypts.

Overleaf: Forest stream in the Otway forests of Victoria.

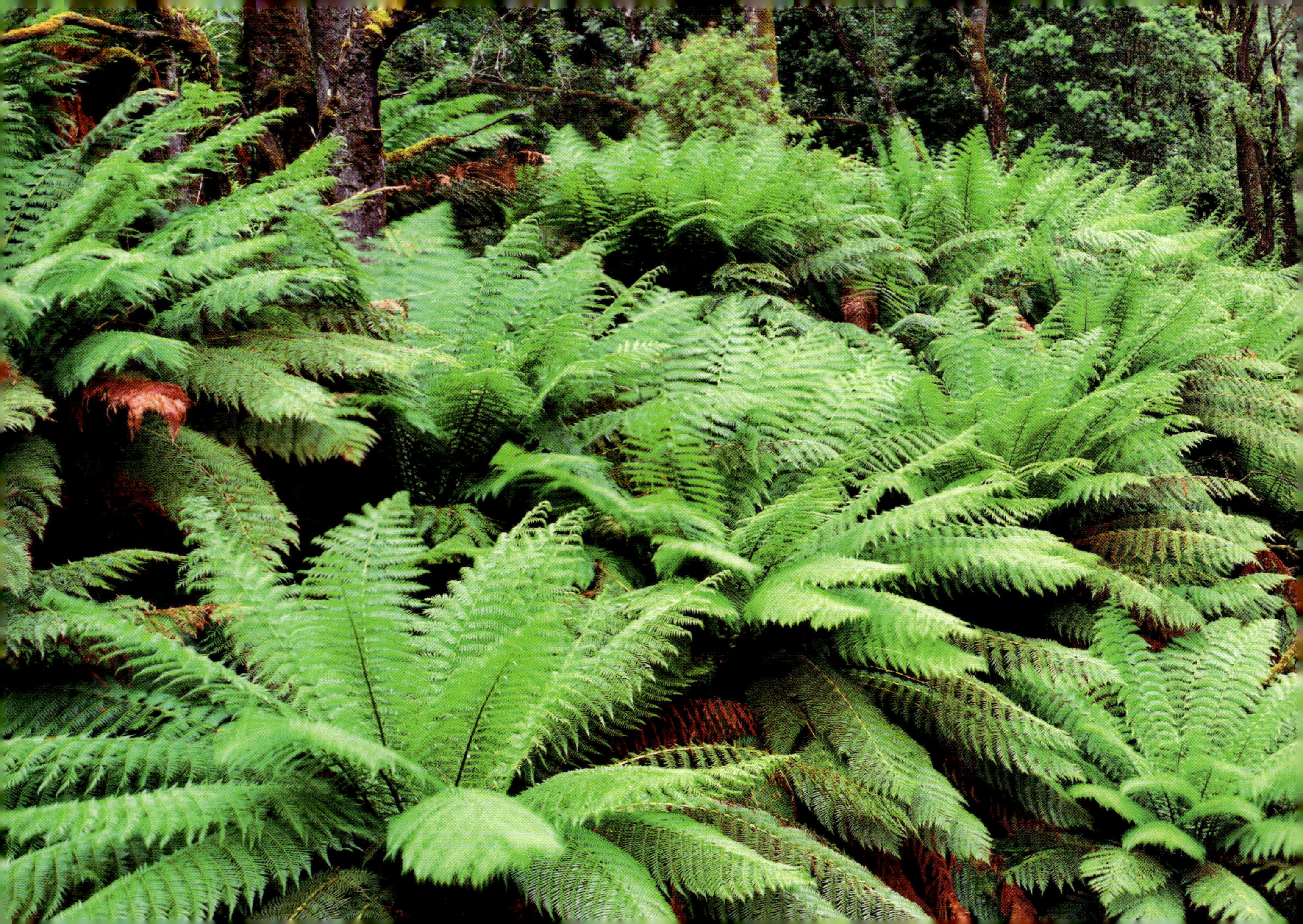

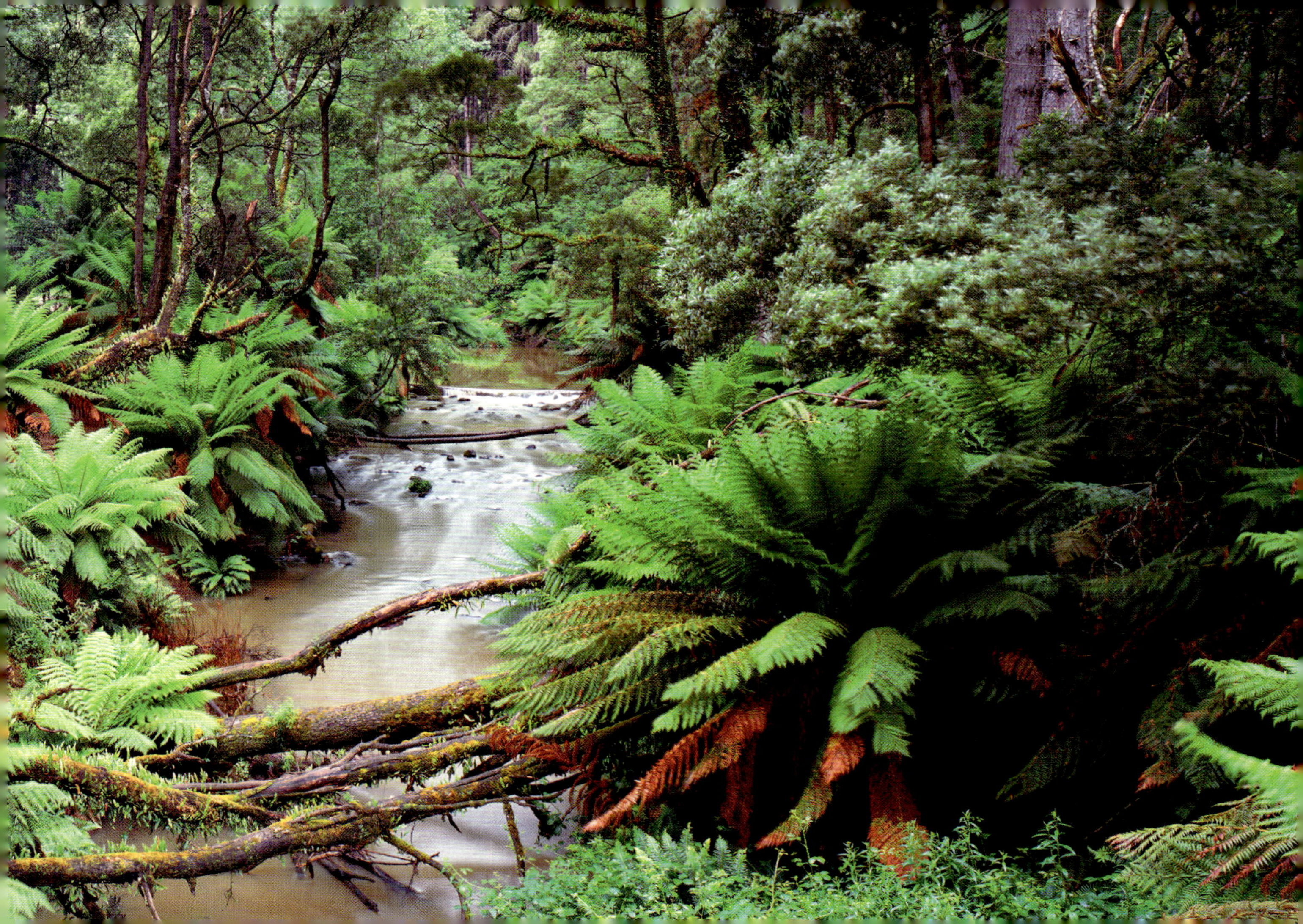

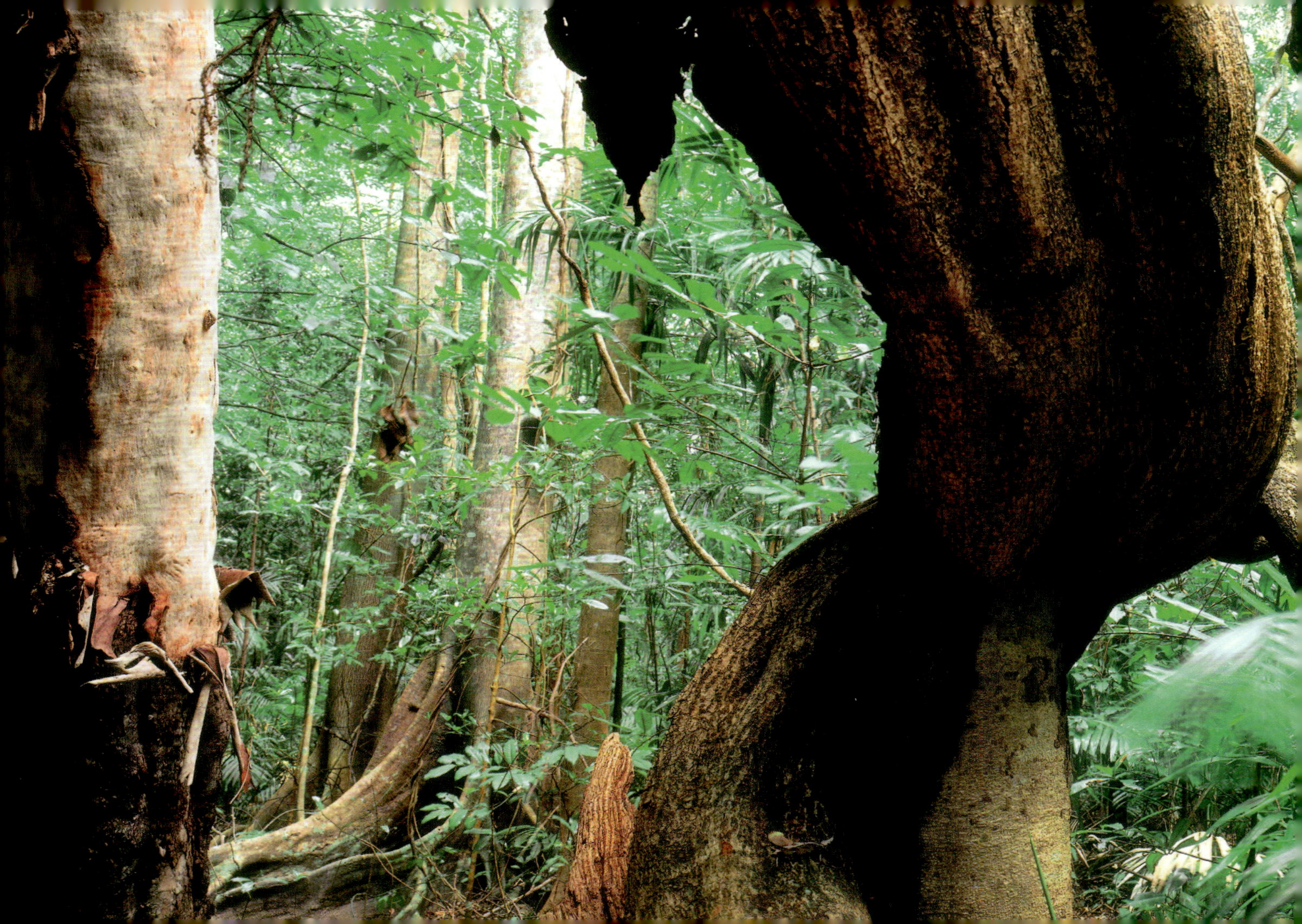

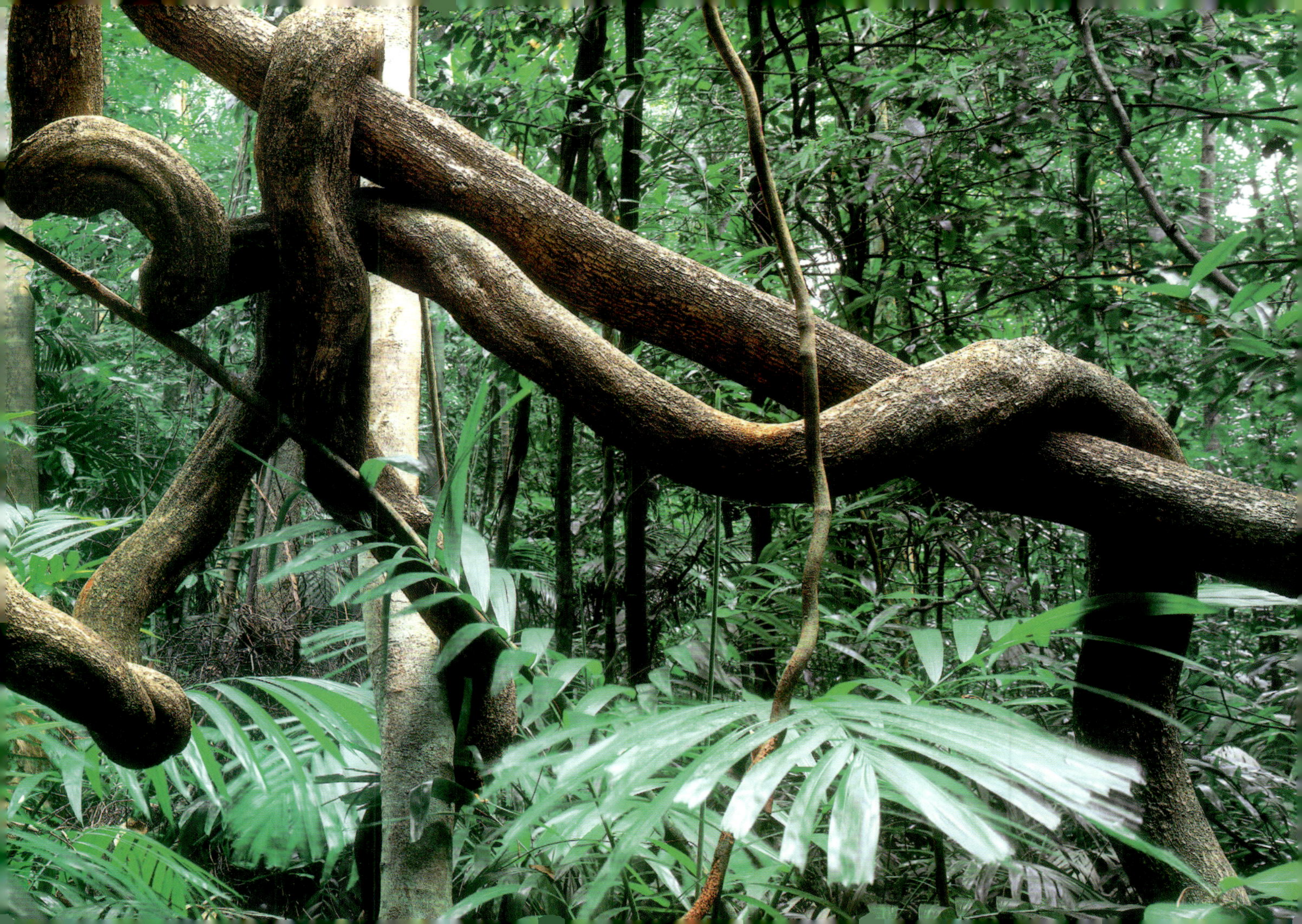

Previous spread: Convoluted vines on Hinchinbrook Island, Qld.   Ancient Antarctic Beech trees within the World Heritage listed rainforests of south-east Queensland.

Clockwise: The rugged rainforest coastline of the Daintree, Qld; the Southern Cassowary, Qld; Mossman Gorge, Qld.

Arching Pendas reach across an unnamed creek on Hinchinbrook Island, Qld.

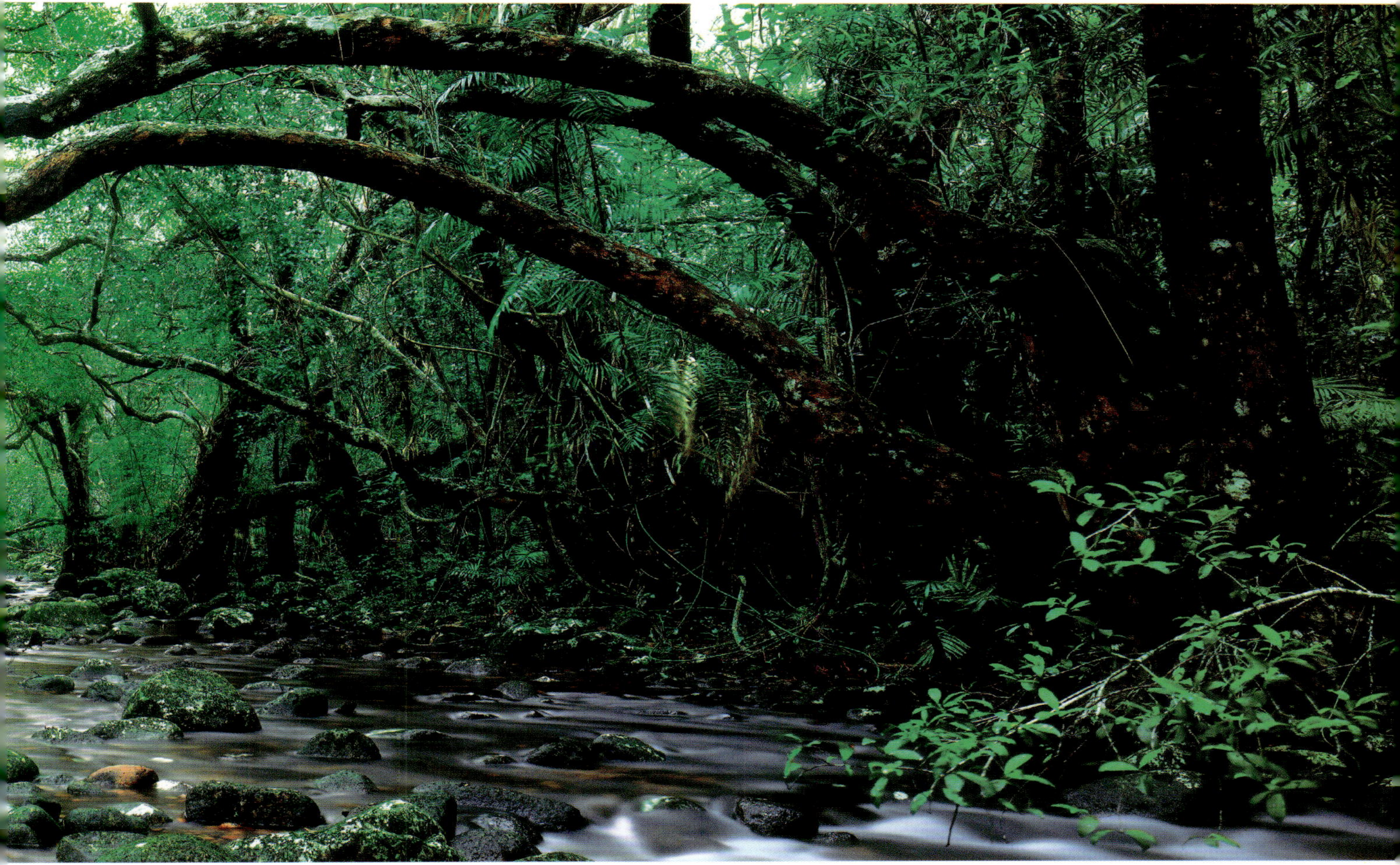

Reflections in Purnululu National Park, W.A.; sand detail on the Kimberley coast, W.A.

The red centre

The arid heart of Australia is home to some of the country's most iconic scenery, from the majestic monolith of Uluru to quirky boulders and swathes of red sand dunes. The limestones and sandstones that form these features owe their origins to a time when water covered the land. Hundreds of millions of years of geological shifting, climate change and erosion have left a dramatic legacy.

From the smallest sand grain to the greatest escarpments, these naturally grey rocks glow rust-red thanks to layers of iron oxide, cemented to the surface by microscopic fungi. By day the landscape burns ochre under the wide, eternally blue sky; at sunset and sunrise it blazes red, pink and mauve.

The arid zone is far from lifeless. Hardy trees and shrubs, with thrifty habits and deep roots, survive on minimal water, prickly, drought-proof spinifex and taking over the most inhospitable terrain. Rare rain fills the riverbeds and transforms the desert with carpets of wild flowers.

White-barked ghost gums cling to ranges; river red gums line dry watercourses nourished by unpredictable floods; ancient palms – remnants of vegetation once widespread when Australia was a wetter place – cling to hidden waterholes. These magical refuges provide havens for rock-wallabies, fishes, frogs, birds and other animals. They are the secret gems of the outback.

A towering Livistona Palm within Mini Palms Gorge, Purnululu National Park, W.A.

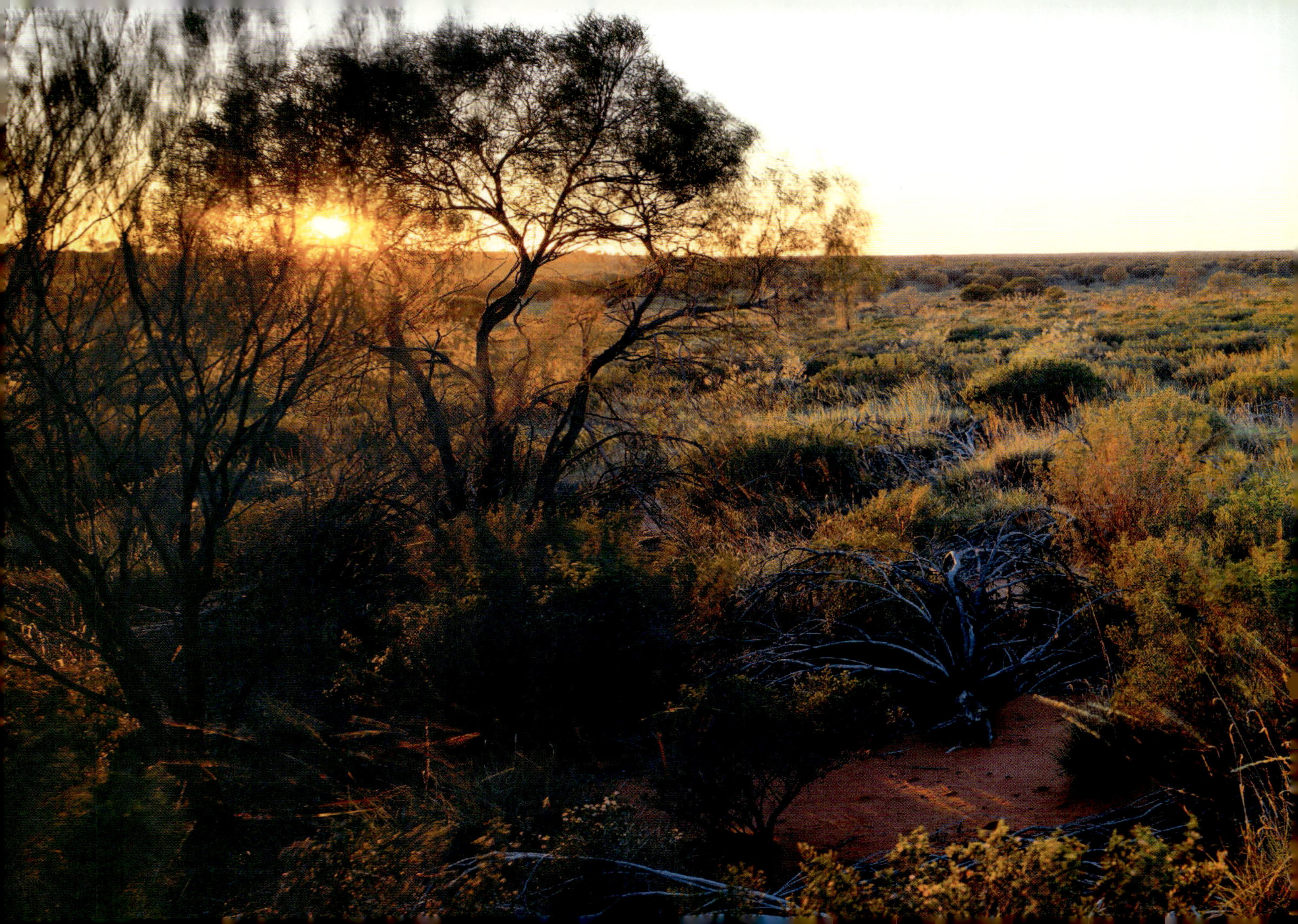

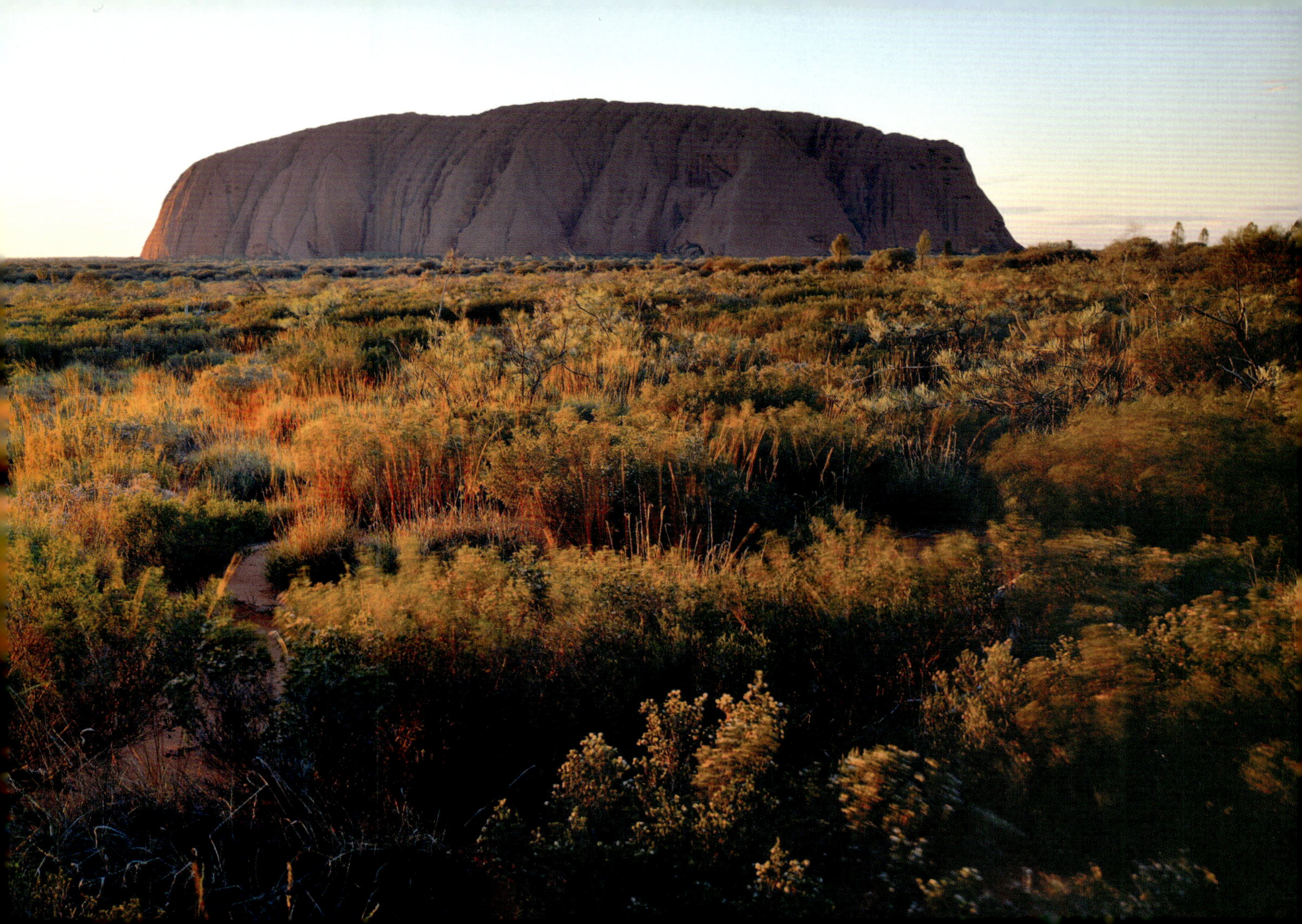

Previous spread: Warm morning light filters across the desert illuminating one of the world's great monoliths, Uluru.

Left: Lichen coloured formations of the Bungle Bungle Range, Purnululu National Park, W.A.
Right: Wildfire in the Kimberley, W.A.

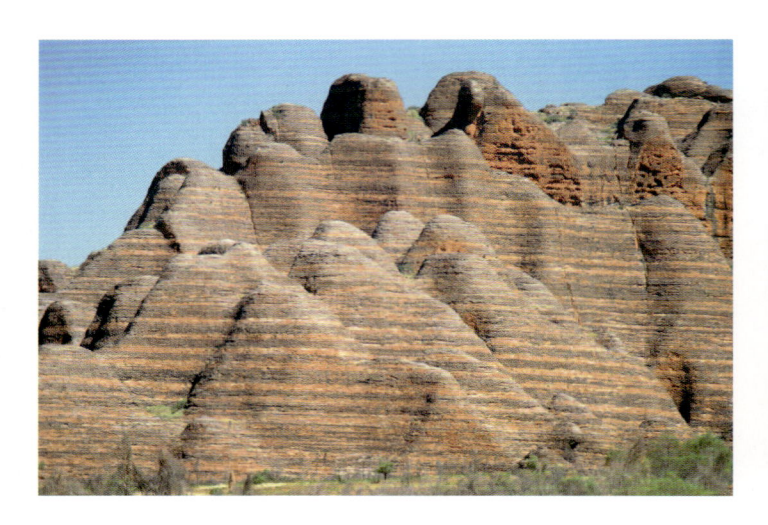

Left: Setting sun over the Mitchell Plateau, Kimberley, W.A.
Right: Bell Gorge, Kimberley, W.A.

Ormiston Gorge, West MacDonnell Ranges, N.T.

Overleaf: Ghost Gum on the rim of Ormiston Pound, N.T.

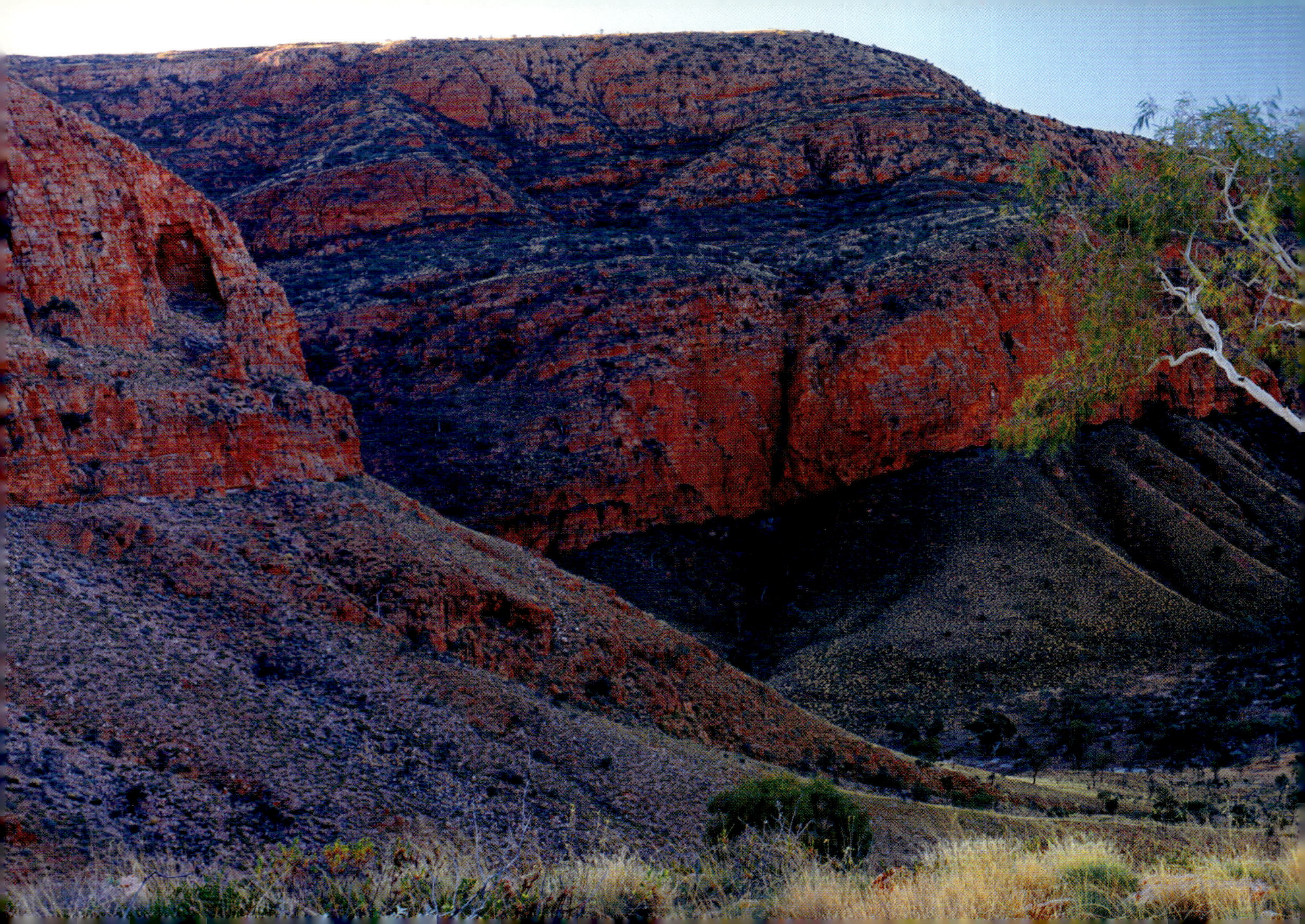

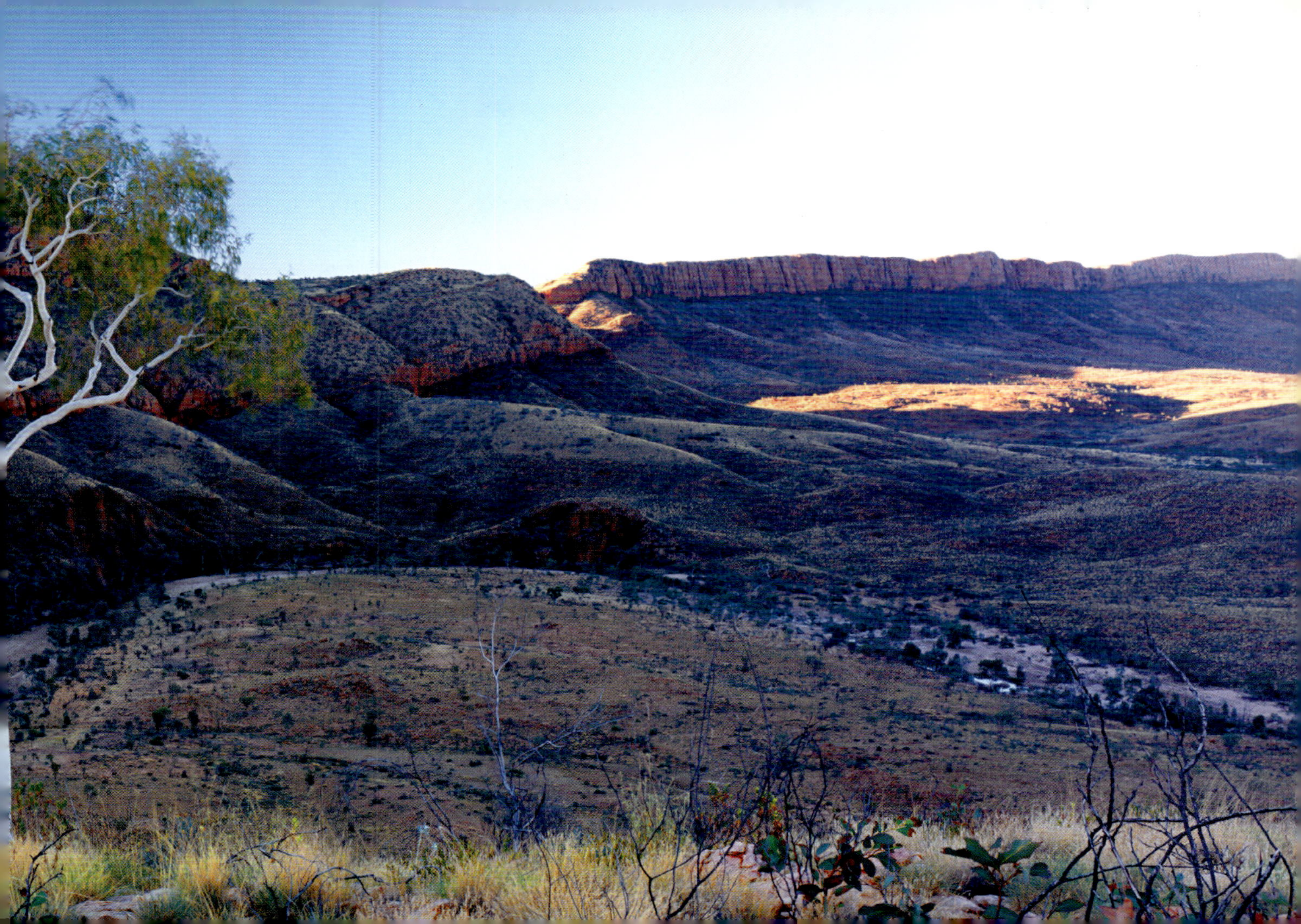

The Three Sisters, Blue Mountains World Heritage Area, NSW.

Stella Martin is a natural history writer living in Cairns, in north Queensland. She is author of Australian Wildlife, published by Bradt Travel Guides in 2010. In 2008 she was presented with a Cassowary Award by the Wet Tropics Management Authority in recognition of her work on Tropical Topics, an educational newsletter on the wildlife of north Queensland, and for her regular Ranger Diary columns in the Cairns Post. In 2006 Stella won second prize in the international BBC Wildlife magazine travel writing competition. **www.stellabridgetmartin.com**

Steven Nowakowski is a leading panoramic photographer. He resides just north of the city of Cairns with his partner and two children. Steven's love of the outdoor life, particularly Australia's remote wilderness areas, has always remained the core and inspiration for his work. Steven has travelled extensively throughout Australia and is a passionate bushwalker who finds sanctity in many of the continent's most hidden and beautiful places - places not viewed by many and only accessible on foot. The Tropical North Queensland region is the most idyllic location for Steven and his family to reside, being surrounded by World Heritage Wet Tropics rainforest, the Great Barrier Reef and the wonders of the Cape York wilderness to the north. Today Steven Nowakowski remains actively involved in numerous environmental campaigns aiming to protect such places. **www.stevennowakowski.com**

Limited Edition Prints, Posters, Calendars and more...
Shop online at **www.stevennowakowski.com.**

The Work Of Time - Cane Cutters Cottage — Limited Edition of 150 only.

Mossman Gorge — Limited Edition of 250 only.

Hinchinbrook Island - a sacred wildness
112 page book featuring 75 panoramic photographs.
Hardcover and softcover versions available

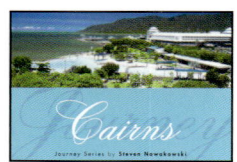

Cairns - Journey Series
64 page book.

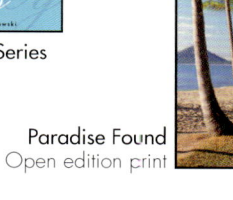

Paradise Found
Open edition print